# Martha Maxwell
## Natural History Pioneer

A NOW YOU  KNOW BIO

James McVey

Filter Press, LLC

Palmer Lake, Colorado

# For Kyle

Cover photo courtesy CU Museum Photograph Collection, X390.

Library of Congress Cataloging-in-Publication Data

McVey, James, 1958-
  Martha Maxwell : natural history pioneer / James McVey.
     p. cm. – (A now you know bio)
  Includes bibliographical references.
   ISBN-13 978-0-86541-075-6 (pbk. : alk. paper)
   1. Maxwell, Martha, 1831-1881—Juvenile literature. 2. Naturalists—Colorado—
Biography—Juvenile literature. 3. Taxidermists—Colorado—Biography—Juvenile lit-
erature. I. Title. II. Series.
   QH31.M36M38 2005
   508.092–dc22
                                        2005027682

Filter Press, LLC, P.O. Box 95, Palmer Lake, Colorado

Printed in the United States of America

# Martha Maxwell

## Natural History Pioneer

# Contents

THE PRAIRIE-DOG'S MOUND.

*Martha Maxwell excelled in taxidermy and developed innovative ways of displaying her specimens in their natural habitats. This display of prairie dogs in Martha's Rocky Mountain Museum was published in* St. Nicholas Magazine *in October 1876.*

# Introduction

This is the story of Martha Maxwell. From the time she was a little girl, she liked to be outdoors with birds and animals. As a young woman, Martha traveled west with her husband on the Oregon Trail to join the Colorado gold rush. In Colorado, she became a well-known **taxidermist**. She created beautiful wildlife displays and built a museum to show them. Her wildlife exhibit at the 1976 Centennial Exposition in Philadelphia made her famous.

Martha is remembered as one of the first taxidermists to display her specimens in a setting that showed animals in their natural **habitats**. She was also the first woman to discover a new **subspecies** of bird, which was later named after her.

Martha believed that a woman could achieve success in any endeavor. Through hard work and perseverance, she found a way to work in the field of **natural history**, even though at the time it was considered for men only. By achieving her goals, she demonstrated to women that they too could follow their dreams.

Many of the quotations in this story are taken from *On the Plains, and Among the Peaks*, a book written about Martha by her sister Mary. Other quotes are taken from newspaper articles, family memoirs, personal letters, and diaries.

*Martha Ann Dartt Maxwell*
*Naturalist, Taxidermist, Museum Builder*

# 1 A Frontier Family

Martha Ann Dart was born in Pennsylvania on July 12, 1831. She lived with her parents on a farm in a town called Dartt's Settlement. Martha's grandparents lived nearby, as did many of her uncles and aunts. The Dartt family had moved west from Connecticut to the Pennsylvania frontier in the late 1820s.

While Martha was still quite young, her mother, Amy, became ill and had to spend much of her time in bed. Then, when Martha was just two-and-a-half years old, her father died of **scarlet fever**. Martha also became sick with the disease, but she soon recovered.

During her mother's illness, Martha grew very close to her Grandmother Abigail. Together they went on long walks in the woods, listening to birds, chasing butterflies, and watching fox and deer. Martha's grandmother knew much about birds and animals, and she taught Martha.

Sometimes at night, Martha and her grandmother studied the animals they had captured in the woods near their home. Grandmother Abigail was a free-spirited woman who taught Martha to love nature and be independent.

Because Martha's mother was not getting better, Grandmother Abigail decided that Amy should return to Connecticut to recover her health. At first, Abigail and Amy planned to take Martha with them, but in the end, Amy decided that Martha should stay in Pennsylvania. "It was quite early in the morning, before I had risen from my bed that she hold me," Martha remembered. "She thought that I had not better go. It was a sad disappointment, and the tears flowed freely for a while."

Martha was just four years old when they left for Connecticut. She lived with relatives, but Martha was lonely with both her mother and grandmother gone. She spent much of her time walking in the woods and caring for the animals around the house. Her mother and grandmother stayed in Connecticut a full year. When they returned to Dartt's Settlement, Martha's mother seemed better.

Because she had no brothers or sisters to play with, Martha spent a lot of time with the family dogs, hens, and livestock. Her special pet was a duckling.

One spring day, it started to rain. Soon the stream near Martha's house grew big, and the current ran fast. As Martha watched, her pet duckling fell into the rushing water. The duckling was pulled under, only to reappear again downstream. Martha followed her duckling along the bank until it disappeared.

"My heart was in great anguish," Martha recalled later. "I cried until mother made me stop for fear it would make me sick. She told me that I had done all I could to save her and that all that could be done now was to pray to God to save her."

That night, Martha prayed as hard as she could. The duckling was her best friend in the whole world. She prayed until she felt certain that her little friend was safe.

The next morning, Martha went looking for her duckling. "I had looked but a short time when I discovered her in a hollow stump in a high bank of the crick [creek] a number of yards up the stream from where she was last seen the evening before, so that she *was* safe sure enough." Martha never forgot her tiny friend and how she prayed for it to be saved.

In addition to learning about animals, Martha learned many things from her mother. "During this time, although mother was unable to take care of herself, she was not negligent in regard to my education. She taught me to read, spell, knit and sew."

When Martha was ten, her mother married a man named Josiah Dartt. Martha was not happy about this at first. "With this change of circumstances I was very much displeased," she wrote later. But her new stepfather wanted to be friends with Martha. Josiah liked to read, and he encouraged Martha to learn.

A year after her marriage to Josiah, Amy gave birth to a baby girl named Mary. Unfortunately, her mother grew ill again, and it was up to Martha to take care of the baby. Over time, Martha and Mary became good friends. Mary remained Martha's best friend throughout her life.

Martha's mother and stepfather were very religious. Josiah had always dreamed of traveling to Oregon to work as a **missionary** among the Indians. One day, they told Martha of their plans to go West.

Martha was thirteen and Mary was two when the family left Pennsylvania in 1844. Josiah planned to spend the winter with Martha's uncles in Illinois before going on to Oregon in the spring. With their belongings piled in two wagons, they traveled across the prairies of Ohio and Indiana.

"We went by land and lived in our wagons night and day," Martha later recalled. "We were five weeks and three days on the road. I never enjoyed five weeks better, I think."

After the family arrived in Illinois, Martha's mother gave birth to a baby girl named Sarah Elizabeth. Once again, Martha had to take over many of the household chores. Soon everyone in the family became sick with chills and fever. They had come down with ague, a malarial infection that was common on the frontier.

Because of their illnesses, it was not possible to go on to Oregon. The family went instead to Wisconsin, where another of Martha's uncles lived. Wisconsin must have suited the family. After living there for two years, Martha's stepfather bought land and built a log cabin in the woods.

There were many challenges to life on the frontier. One day, while Josiah was away, Martha heard a buzzing sound coming from the unfinished part of the house. Martha and her mother rushed to the doorway. A large rattlesnake was coiled near little Mary. It was ready to strike!

Mary later described how Martha saved her life. "Quick as thought she sprang and caught the child, gave it to her mother, and seizing her father's every ready gun, placed it across some rails not far from the reptile, aimed and fired, sending it mangled and dying into the cellar!"

When Josiah came home and heard what had happened, he knew it was time to teach Martha the proper way to handle a rifle. Martha quickly learned how to load and shoot.

When she was sixteen, Martha's family moved to a town called Baraboo. Her stepfather worked at the general store and the family lived in a cozy house next door. This was a happy time for the family. During the evenings, Josiah played his flute and Martha sang. Sometimes young men from the town joined in the singing. Martha was nearly all grown-up now. She was not very tall, less than five feet. She had brown hair and blue eyes. Josiah loved to see her dimples when she smiled.

The family had been in Baraboo for only a few months when Martha's mother became ill again. As before, most of the household chores fell to Martha. All day long, she was busy cooking, cleaning, and caring for her two younger sisters. At night, though, after Mary and "Lizzie" went to bed, Josiah would read to Martha while her mother sewed. He read about current affairs from the *New York Tribune*, and they often discussed politics. Josiah could see that Martha was a bright young woman. Later, he would tell Martha that it was "the great desire of my heart—that you might get a good education."

The town clergyman, the Reverend Cochran, suggested that Martha attend Oberlin College in Ohio. Oberlin was the first college in the United States to admit women as well as men. Josiah liked the idea of Martha earning a college degree. He and Amy agreed that Martha would attend Oberlin in the spring.

# 2 A Year at Oberlin

Before she left for college, Martha's mother took her to the dressmaker to order a **trousseau** and new bonnet for the trip. Mary remembered the bonnet "was covered with a soft queer-woven blue and white silk with folds of the same for trimming! We thought Mattie looked lovely in the new things."

In April 1851, Martha boarded a wagon and took her seat next to the men passengers. As the team of horses pulled away, she waved good-bye to her family. Martha planned to ride the coach one hundred miles to Milwaukee, where she could board a steamship across Lake Michigan to New Buffalo. From there, she would take a train to Detroit and board another steamship across Lake Erie to Cleveland. From Cleveland, she could take a train to Wellington, Ohio, and then another stagecoach to Oberlin.

On the first day of her trip, Martha noticed that one of the horses was limping. The second day, the driver—a man named Fowler—whipped the team and refused to feed the horses. When the limping horse could hardly walk, the driver whipped the animal until it fell to the ground. Then he rode off to look for another horse. While he was gone, another coach came down the road. The driver offered to take the passengers in his wagon, so they loaded their bags in his coach and started down the road.

That night, Fowler caught up with the wagon. He told the passengers that he had found a new team of horses and could now take them to Milwaukee, if they didn't mind riding through the night.

"I told him I did not want to ride with any man who would abuse a horse as he abused his," Martha later told her parents. "I thought it best for me to go with the other man. I told him too that I was willing to pay him for my ride as far as I rode with him. This was the opinion of all the men. I asked him what he charged. He said two dollars. This, said I, is too much considering all the disappointment, loss of time, and trouble we have had. I talked with the other passengers about it. They said, 'Don't you pay it. It is not right. We won't. We will pay him fifty cents and that is all we will pay.'"

When Fowler asked for two dollars, Martha offered to pay him fifty cents. "I will have two dollars or nothing," he said. "Very well," said Martha, and paid the man nothing.

After a week of traveling, Martha arrived in Oberlin to begin college. She was nineteen years old. At Oberlin, Martha studied history, mathematics, Latin, and natural science. Sometimes she grew homesick for her family in Baraboo, but she made many friends and enjoyed social events at the college.

Oberlin set strict study hours for its students. If Martha wanted to take a walk in the woods, which she loved to do, she had to get permission from the principal. The college also had a rule that limited public speaking by women. This discrimination against women bothered Martha. Even so, she was happy at Oberlin. She worked hard and was an excellent student, especially in natural science. She devoted her spare time to social **reform** groups that worked against slavery and against the use of tobacco. She also taught Sunday school in her free time.

Martha had time for social clubs, too. She sang in the school choir, enjoyed sleigh rides, and attended parties. Martha liked that men and women could attend college together. In her diary she wrote, "How much more pleasant, animating, and beneficial for students of both sexes to be educated together, and to associate together." Martha became close friends with one young man in particular. They went on walks together, and she told him all about herself.

As time went on, it became clear that Martha's family could not afford to keep her at Oberlin. Martha was disappointed, but she understood. It cost a lot of money to attend college. After only one year, Martha left Oberlin and returned to Baraboo. She wrote in her diary, "O! how has fancy winged hope sunk like a leaden wait [weight] to the bottom of the deep waters of my heart." Martha missed being a student.

In November 1853, Martha started a job as a teacher. She taught young students in a small log cabin outside of Baraboo. The schoolhouse had a dirt floor. The first thing she did was organize her students to clean the room and gather firewood for the stove. When she had the cabin in order, Martha taught her students reading, writing, and arithmetic.

That spring, Martha's family bought a farm near Baraboo. The farm was called Pewitt's Nest. It had a pretty

## Know More!

There was a time in the United States when only men could go to college. When Martha was born, there were no colleges that admitted women. She was lucky. Oberlin College opened its doors in 1833. It was co-educational from the start. That is, both men and women were admitted. Find examples of other trailblazing women scholars. Who was the first woman to receive a medical degree? How about a law degree? Where were they educated? When was the first women's college established and where?

white house beside a spring and many fine trees. To help buy the farm, Martha donated the money from the sale of her share of the family land back in Pennsylvania. She had been saving the money for Oberlin, but it was important that her family have a house of their own. While she still hoped to finish college one day, it looked less and less likely that she would ever return to Oberlin.

# 3

# A Change of Plans

In the summer of 1853, Martha received an interesting offer from one of the richest men in Baraboo. James Maxwell owned a general store, a grist mill, and a number of farms. He was a tall man about the same age as Martha's stepfather. Mr. Maxwell asked Martha if she would **chaperone** his two oldest children at Lawrence University in Appleton, Wisconsin. In return, he would pay for Martha to take classes. Martha agreed to go. At Lawrence, she would be able to resume her studies without worrying about money.

In the fall, she and Mr. Maxwell traveled to Appleton with his children, Emma and Jim. They found a room for Martha and Emma to share. Young Jim took a room in a **boardinghouse** nearby.

Martha was very happy to be back in college. She enrolled in classes in math, natural philosophy, and drawing. She worked for a women's magazine and the

Young Ladies Mutual Improvement Association. Right away, she noticed that clothing styles were different in Appleton. Many young women wore "bloomers," an outfit consisting of a jacket, skirt, and trousers. Martha liked the style. It was much more practical than the long dresses she was used to wearing.

One day, Martha received a surprising letter from Mr. Maxwell. She could hardly believe what it said. "It is both my *interest* and my *inclination* to marry again when the *proper* time comes round," Mr. Maxwell wrote, "provided it brings with it an arrangement with a suitable person."

As she read, it became clear that Mr. Maxwell wanted to marry *her*. Martha had no idea what to think. She was only twenty-two. Mr. Maxwell was twenty years older. And his children! He had six children, the youngest, Gussie, was only six years old. A short time later, Mr. Maxwell wrote again with the same proposal. She wrote back that she needed to discuss the matter with her mother.

At Christmastime, Martha returned to Baraboo and told her parents about the proposal. Josiah thought that James Maxwell would be a good husband for Martha. Amy thought Martha should make up her own mind. Mr. Maxwell was a respected gentleman who seemed to genuinely care for Martha. But would marriage mean giving up her studies again? And how would she care for his children?

Martha returned to Lawrence not knowing what to do. She wasn't sure she wanted to marry, but before long she came to a decision. She agreed to marry James, and the wedding took place in Appleton on March 30, 1854.

Shortly after the wedding, Martha returned to the Dartt farm in Baraboo, where several letters had arrived for her. "One she seized and opened and read with a face growing white," her sister Mary remembered, "I was watching her and shall never forget her face as she crushed it into her pocket and moved away like one in a dream."

Mary later learned what had happened. After she left Oberlin, Martha had written several letters to a young man. She waited anxiously for a reply, but no letter ever came. According to Mary, Martha thought "he did not care for her and was so blue over it she felt quite desperate and that nothing mattered much what she did. If all her friends wanted her to mary Mr. Maxwell she would better do so."

But her special friend at Oberlin *had* replied to her letters. "For some unexplained reason," Mary continued, "her letters had reached him but none of his had come to her. In this one he had told her of his love for her and begged her to continue to write him and to let him hope that soon he could claim her for life!"

Martha's Oberlin friend wanted to marry her, but what could she do? Martha knew that she could not go back on

*James Maxwell, Martha's husband, was a widower with six children when he and Martha married in 1854.*

her promise. She was married to James now, and she must honor her wedding vows.

Marriage to James brought new challenges. When Martha moved in the Maxwells, the house was dirty and the children were not well. Little Gussie suffered from sores caused by lice. Martha had to care for four children plus James and his father. To make matters worse, the children sometimes resented her for having married their father.

With all the cooking, cleaning, and child care, she had little time for herself. But Martha was not one to let go of her ambitions. After all, she came from a family of independent women. Martha joined several social reform movements such as the abolition movement, women's suffrage, and temperance. The abolition movement worked to abolish slavery. Women's suffrage sought to give women the right to vote, and the temperance movement worked to end the use of alcohol.

In addition to her **activism**, Martha showed a talent for creating natural arrangements. One year, she won two awards at the county fair for the best cage of canaries and the best collection of houseplants.

Her relationship with the Maxwell children improved, but Martha wanted a child of her own. Her desire was fulfilled on November 17, 1857, when her daughter was born. Martha's only child was named Mabel.

Two years later, James was forced to sell his mill and many of his properties. The nation's economy was in a **depression**, and James lost much of his wealth. When gold was discovered in Colorado, the headlines of the Baraboo newspaper read, *"Ho! For Pike's Peak!"* James wanted to seek his fortune in Colorado. His son Alonzo was already there. James told Martha he planned to join the gold rush.

James must have been surprised when Martha said she would go, too. Ever since Oberlin, Martha had wanted to make something of her life. She wanted to be more than a wife and homemaker. In the West, she might have the chance to do that.

At first, James protested. After all, there was Mabel to care for. In the end, there was little James could do to change Martha's mind. Two-year-old Mabel would be left in the care of Martha's mother and sisters. Just as her mother had left her as a child, Martha now left Mabel.

# 4 Colorado Gold Camps

In the spring of 1860, the Maxwells prepared for their journey west. James bought two **Conestoga wagons** that they loaded with six months' supply of clothes, blankets, cooking utensils, molasses, applesauce, dried beef, and twenty bushels of potatoes and onions. At least three other men from Baraboo decided to go with them.

On a cold spring day, the wagons pulled out of Baraboo. James wanted to start the journey before the roads became clogged with mud. At first, Martha and James slept in local taverns while the other men slept in a tent. But Martha enjoyed being outdoors, so she and James used a sheet to divide the tent into two rooms and slept there. They made a bed by putting down hay and covering it with blankets.

Martha cooked for the men on a small camp stove. She fried potatoes and onions along with ducks and prairie chickens the men hunted during the day. To bake bread, she used a **Dutch oven** that was placed directly on the campfire coals. She described the camp in one of her letters home:

> If you wish to know where I am, just imagine you see me seated on a wooden pail instead of a chair beside me a writing desk composed of first, a trunk for the base, next a pail for the stand and, last a tinpan bottomside up for the top…Around in every direction there is nothing for the eye to rest upon but an uneven surface of brown monotony, except now and then an isolated house or a lonely craggy tree upon an elevated part of the bald Prairie.

In another letter, she described what happened when one of the wooden axles broke on the wagon while she was driving the horses. "I suggested to James that I considered him capable of facing any immergency and had no doubt the thing would be fixed up without much delay, 'And you are not going to try to mend the matter by sheding a pint or so of tears?' he answered Of course, I replyed in the negative, for you know I've but little *faith* in that remedy."

It took them three weeks to reach Omaha, Nebraska. After a short rest, the group started west again, this time following the Platte River. They were on the Great Plains now, and there were fewer trees. Prairie grasses covered the rolling hills as far as the eye could see. Big cottonwood trees grew along the winding river, which was shallow and wide, with many sandbars.

Some nights, James played his **melodeon** around the campfire. Another man played the flute, and the rest of the group sang. Sometimes Martha heard coyotes and wolves howling in the dark. The sky seemed bigger and wider, with thousands of shining stars.

The further west they went, the muddier the trail seemed to get. Many other wagons were on the trail, and their tracks stretched clear to the horizon. In some places, the wheel ruts grew deep and the going was slow. The Maxwell party was joined by five other wagons. Martha was the only woman in the entire group.

The saw fewer and fewer houses. The houses they did see were made of sod cut from the ground. Martha described these **sod houses** in a letter home. "I am writing in the wagon on my lap, the wind blows in a manner you know nothing about and dust flies in clouds. For the last 100 miles most of the houses and fences are built of sod cut in the shape of brick and put up in the same manner minus the mortar."

Martha was fascinated by the Indians they encountered along the Oregon Trail. "Their manner of conversing by signs, their ornaments amuse me vastly," she wrote.

In another letter she described an Indian burial site. "A few days since, we passed, the grave of an Indian Chief, which was surrounded by a circle of horses' heads (the bones) 57 in number. The Chief owned the horses and they were killed for his use in the Spirit Land."

Martha even wrote that an Indian "proposed buying me, or swapping three ponys for me." She joked that she might have liked the trade.

Martha was also fascinated by the new animal **species** she saw. She was especially interested in the antelope and prairie dogs. The prairie dogs stood up on their hind legs when the wagons passed by, as though they were watching a parade.

When Martha saw the Rocky Mountains at last, she wrote, "I thought that I could imagine something how Columbus felt when he discovered America as after a month's monotonous journeying over a sea of land, we saw looming up silvery and beautiful in the robes of eternal white the objects of our search."

After two months of traveling across the Great Plains, the wagon train reached Denver, a busy settlement of log cabins and tents. The Maxwells set up camp on the banks of Cherry Creek and prepared for their journey into the mountains. In Denver, Martha met an old friend from Wisconsin named Mary Cawker. The two women agreed to be partners and run a boardinghouse in the mining district. They bought property together in Mountain City, a mining camp located thirty-five miles west of Denver.

James's son Alonzo had been in the mountains for some time already. He met the family in Denver, and they all started for Mountain City. When they arrived at the camp, Martha was surprised to see so many people. Gold miners were everywhere. The Maxwells found a place to pitch their tent and set up camp.

James and his sons quickly learned to pan for gold. They left Martha at the camp and went into the mountains to **stake a claim**. While they were gone, Martha earned money by washing and mending clothes and baking pies for the miners.

The men returned without finding any gold, so Martha hired her husband to build a boardinghouse on the property that she and Mary Cawker had bought. In only a few weeks, the two-story house was finished. It had one room on the top floor and a bedroom and living room below.

Martha and Mary's boardinghouse made money, but by August Martha had sold her share. She and James moved to a new camp called Nevada City, where James built a much larger boardinghouse with a dining hall. James and his sons continued to search for gold but without much success.

In the winter, James was hired to go to Iowa to drive a herd of cattle west. Martha remained at her new boardinghouse—cooking, cleaning, and washing clothes for miners. Sometimes she had as many as seventy-five miners staying at the boardinghouse. It was hard work, but

Martha was making money. In fact, she was making more money than all the other family members combined.

Martha liked the independence that a steady income brought. She saved her money and bought a **squatter's claim** downstream from Denver on the Platte River. The property had a one-room cabin. Her squatter's claim required that someone had to live in the cabin if she was to own the property one day. Members of the Maxwell family took turns staying at the cabin until it became legally hers.

*New towns sprang up as miners moved into the mountains of Colorado in search of gold. Nevada City, shown in this 1864 photograph, was where James hoped to strike it rich and where Martha opened a boardinghouse in 1860.*

In the spring of 1861, James returned to Baraboo to pick up Gussie and Josiah and take them to Colorado. Martha decided Mabel was still too young to make the journey west. Josiah and Bussie lived with the Maxwells at the boardinghouse in Nevada City.

When she wasn't working, Martha loved to hike in the mountains above town and watch the animals and birds. As she had done at Oberlin, she joined a temperance group that also supported women's suffrage. She also hosted parties. A newspaper reporter from the *Rocky Mountain News* wrote an article about one of her parties. "[A] fine social party was given Tuesday evening last in Mrs. Maxwell's hall…Everything went of[f] in splendid style. The management was good, music excellent, and the supper got up in her own best style by the charming hostess."

## Know More!

### BOOM and BUST

Gold was discovered in Nevada City in 1859. Within two weeks, 10,000 people had 'rushed' to the area. The gold rush towns sprung up, grew quickly, and then faded into ghost towns. Locate Colorado's ghost towns in a book or travel guide. Are the ghost towns included on modern maps? Which county has the most abandoned towns? Have any of the towns been restored?

Josiah and Gussie returned to Baraboo at the end of the summer. It was an uncertain time. The nation drew closer to the **Civil War.** Men from both the North and the South lived in the mining district. No one knew what would happen if war broke out. Many miners went back east to be with their families. Every day, it seemed, more and more miners left Nevada City.

Then in the fall, disaster struck. A fire started in the forest above Nevada City and quickly spread through the town. Fifty houses burned to the ground, including Martha's boardinghouse. Martha and James lost nearly all their belongings.

After the fire, Martha and James decided not to rebuild. Instead, they went to Lump Gulch, where James had a cabin on his mining claim. But winter was approaching, and neither wanted to be in the mountains during the cold weather. So, they left the mining district and moved to the cabin on the squatter's claim near Denver. There they could begin farming in the spring.

When Martha and James arrived at the ranch, they were surprised to find three strangers living in the cabin. The strangers had claimed the ranch for their own and had no intention of leaving.

The next day, the Maxwells went to the land office in Denver to request a hearing to prove the property was theirs. The judge who heard their case ruled in their favor.

Still, the claim jumpers refused to leave. The men said it was theirs now, and they planned to stay.

One of the claim jumpers had animal and bird specimens mounted in the cabin. Martha was immediately fascinated by what she saw. She asked the German man who had prepared the specimens to teach her how to do this. The man agreed to teach her for ten dollars a lesson, beginning the next day.

When Martha returned for her lesson, the man told her that he had changed his mind. Martha asked why and was told it was because she was a woman. He was afraid that she would become so good and preserving animals that she would take all his business.

"Vimin is besser as men mit den hands in shmall verks" the German man said. "Ven you know dis pisness you makes de pirds and peasts so quicker as I; you leave me no more verk at all! Es is besser fur me I keeps vat I knows mit mineself."

Martha promised him that she would not take his business, but he still refused to teach her. Martha was furious. If this man would not teach her taxidermy, then she would certainly not allow him to say in her cabin! But how could she get him to leave? She came up with a plan.

Martha learned from her neighbors that the German man liked to play cards at a stage stop on the other side of the river. Alonzo helped her watch the cabin for a week, until one day they saw the man leave. When he was out of sight, Martha hurried to the cabin.

"Withdrawing the staple, which held the padlock, from the door-frame, she entered," Mary later wrote, "and carefully gathering up his earthly effects, removed them to a convenient point on the plains, where she left them in a neat pile."

After they removed the man's belongings, Martha and Alonzo barricaded the door from inside. That night when the man returned, he banged on the door and tried to break it down. Alonzo drew his pistol and fired into the air until the man left. The next day the German returned and hauled away his belongings. Martha had saved the ranch. Now the family could begin farming.

Before removing the man's possessions from the cabin, Martha had studied the German's specimens. She noticed all the materials and tools he used to prepare the bird and animal bodies. Later, Martha wrote to her family in Baraboo and asked them to send a book on taxidermy. "I wish to learn how to preserve birds and other animal curiosities in this country," she wrote.

# 5 A Talent for Taxidermy

In November 1862, Martha left her adventurous life in the West and returned to Wisconsin. Her sister Mary had written that their mother was ill, and the family needed Martha at Pewit's Nest to help care for her and Mabel.

It had been nearly three years since Martha had last seen her daughter, yet she was surprised to discover that Mabel called Amy "mother." Mabel was five now and growing up fast.

Mary was enrolled at a school in Baraboo called Collegiate Institute. One day, she came to Martha with some exciting news. Professor Hobart, the principal, wanted to start a collection of stuffed birds for the school. "We must have a Department of Zoology," he told the students. "Can't some of you young ladies who have more skilful fingers than I, assist me in putting up some birds?"

*Martha and James had one child, a daughter named Mabel. She was born in 1857. As a child, Mabel did not like the attention that her mother gave to hunting and taxidermy. As an adult, Mabel had a closer relationship with her mother.*

Mary and Elizabeth told Professor Hobart they knew just the right person to help with the collection.

Martha was not sure about the idea at first. She didn't have any experience with mounting birds. But she told Mary she would speak with the professor. Martha was surprised to learn that the professor knew even less about taxidermy than she did. So she agreed to help. She read everything she could find on the subject. Martha had a friend, Mr. Ogden, who liked to mount the various birds he hunted. She paid him a visit and examined the specimens he kept in his parlor. They weren't as beautiful as the German's, but as least Mr. Ogden was willing to teach Martha what he knew.

Martha helped Professor Hobart prepare bird specimens for the school. In those days, taxidermists mounted birds by skinning them, then stuffing wood shavings inside the skin. They shaped the body until it looked right and then sewed the skin together. The head, wings, and tail feathers were wired into place before the bird was finally attached to its perch.

Once, Martha and the professor were having trouble mounting a bird. They could not get the bird's rumpled feathers to lay flat, no matter what they tried. Martha had an idea. "We'll get a nest and put the bird up fighting!" she said. "Of course, in that case, it would be all bristled up, and its feathers standing every way." Martha and the professor found a nest and mounted a second bird so it looked like the mother bird was defending her home.

Martha worked hard at her new craft. She studied the birds around her house, watching to see how they stood on a branch, tilted their heads, and crouched down before taking off to fly. This helped her to shape and mount specimens to look like real birds. She discovered that if she spread the wings out a little, the bird looked as if it was getting ready to fly. If she cocked the head to one side, the bird looked as if it was listening.

Martha placed some of her bird specimens in the plants that her mother kept in the parlor. She also put grass on the cabinet where Josiah kept his collection of fossils and minerals. In the grass, she placed two red squirrels. One of the squirrels was eating a butternut. On the lower shelf of the cabinet, she arranged a family of ducks and a weasel that watched them from behind a rock.

Martha helped out at the school for two years. It was 1864, and the nation was fighting the Civil War. Martha volunteered her time to the Union cause. She also worked for the Loyal Women's League of Baraboo. The group wanted the U.S. Congress to pass an act that would give freedom to all Americans, including slaves.

In the spring of 1865, Martha and Mabel moved from Pewit's Nest to the Maxwell house in Baraboo. Once again, Martha had to take care of the entire Maxwell household. As time went on, she grew tired and unhappy. Unable to pursue her own interests and exhausted from taking care of so many people, Martha decided to enter the new Battle Creek **Sanitarium** in Michigan, where she could rest and recover her health.

Martha stayed at Battle Creek from September 1866 through the following spring. After months of healthy food, exercise, and rest, she returned to Baraboo with her health restored and her spirit renewed. But she knew she must find a way to do the things that made her happy. She had heard about a new town back east that sounded like a good place to live. So in 1867, she and Mabel moved to Vineland, New Jersey.

Vineland was a community built on idealistic principles. The town had houses and schools and stores like any other town, but the people who lived there were dedicated to many of the social causes that Martha had been involved in, including temperance and women's rights. Martha bought a house in Vineland where she and Mabel could live.

Meanwhile, James had sold the ranch near Denver and built two sawmills near Boulder, where he and his sons worked. He hadn't seen Martha or Mabel in over four years. James was not happy that his wife and daughter had moved to New Jersey, and he asked Martha to return to Colorado. When Martha refused to leave Vineland, James traveled across the country to try to persuade her. In the end, Martha agreed to return to Colorado.

The Maxwells—James, Martha, and Mabel—traveled west in the spring of 1868. Martha's sister Mary decided to join them on the trip.

It had been eight years since Martha and James first came west on the Oregon Trail. This time, the family took a train all the way to Cheyenne, Wyoming. Because of a recent Indian attack, the Maxwells had to wait in Cheyenne for an army escort. They eventually rode to Boulder in a carriage under the protection of the cavalry.

Martha loved the natural beauty of her new home. Boulder was located in a valley at the foot of the mountains, with a creek that ran through town. James rented a house in the country for the family. Martha liked the location of the house, Mary wrote, because she "wanted to be out of doors where she could study the animal life and get specimens to mount."

Martha was eager to resume her work in taxidermy. She wanted to collect as many native Colorado birds and animals as she could. "It seemed especially desirable this work be done," Mary said, "from the fact that the strange and curious animals peculiar to its plains and mountains were rapidly disappearing."

At first, Martha depended on James and the local boys to bring her animals and birds. Sometimes, while hiking alone, she would see an animal she wanted to collect. Because she did not have a gun, she was not able to hunt it. If she learned to shoot well, she could collect specimens herself.

It took some time for Martha to become a good shot. First of all, she handled the gun in an unusual way. She held it to her right shoulder and aimed with her left eye. James teased her about this strange way of taking aim. He stopped teasing her when he discovered that she could shoot as well as he could.

Some animals and birds were difficult for Martha to work on. The turkey vulture was one. Vultures were **scavengers** that ate dead and rotting carcasses. Martha's vulture smelled so bad that she knew she couldn't work on it in the house. She took it outside to the creek bank. Even there, the smell was so awful that Mabel and Mary complained from the house.

When she cut the bird's skin open and started to clean it, Martha thought she would faint. She had to walk away. Even though the odor was awful, Martha knew she must have a specimen for her collection. Vultures were important birds in the natural order of things. Mary later wrote, "It was more than a week, however, before she recovered from the effects of such a disgusting task enough to be able to eat an ordinary meal; and it was many weeks before the mounted bird could be taken from the outer shed, that gave him shelter, and have a place among the other birds."

In addition to collecting species and working on her taxidermy skills, Martha wanted to learn more about

*Martha was an excellent hunter. She and her spaniel often spent days camping and hunting animals for her museum.*

animals and birds. She read books about Colorado wildlife and studied the behavior of animals in the wild. When she cleaned her specimens, she studied the **anatomy** of each animal. She also paid close attention to the habitats of the birds and animals she collected. Her love for nature made it easy for her to learn about natural history.

The Maxwell house was soon filled with Martha's specimens. There were owls and hawks in the parlor and foxes and rabbits in the kitchen. The larger specimens were stored in the shed.

James helped Martha, but Mabel did not like anything about her mother's hobby. She felt that Martha spent too much time with her animals. "I was bitterly jealous of the animals that seemed to absorb all the interest and affection for which I longed," she remembered.

When Martha went on hunting trips, Mabel was left at home to keep house for her father. "How I did it I can't imagine," she later wrote. "My mother was not at all domestic and there was no one to teach me."

# 6 Building Her Collection

In the fall of 1868, the Colorado Agricultural Society held its annual exhibition in Denver. Martha thought this would be a good opportunity to show her collection So she organized all her animals and birds and prepared them for her first public exhibition.

People from all over Colorado Territory came to see the exhibits. Everyone seemed to like Martha's display. "The largest collection of Colorado birds we have ever seen is now on exhibition at the Fair Grounds," said the *Rocky Mountain News.* "They were picked up by Mrs. Maxwell, of Boulder, within six months, count over one hundred different kinds, and are arranged on two large shrubs of cottonwood with a great deal of taste."

Martha displayed hummingbirds, eagles, prairie chickens, and hawks. On the final day of the fair, Martha won the award for best display in natural history. The judges gave her a fifty dollar prize! They thought her specimens were beautiful and well crafted. They especially liked how she placed her birds in a realistic setting.

Martha had found her calling. Her artistry and skill had won her recognition. But she was far from satisfied. She knew that to be a top-notch naturalist, she must learn more about science. In 1869, she wrote to the Smithsonian Institution in Washington, D.C., and asked the scientists there to recommend books. She also mentioned that she had a number of birds in her collection that she could not identify.

Martha received a reply from one of the scientists. He suggested a book and invited her to send her specimens. "If there are any birds in your collection that you cannot identify, and will send them to us by mail, Prof. Baird will determine them for you," the letter read. Martha was thrilled to hear from the Smithsonian. In the years ahead, she became friends with the scientists there and sent them many specimens.

Martha was determined to be the best taxidermist and naturalist she could be. She went on long hikes to observe animals and birds in the wild. Sometime she stayed out all day. When she hunted, she took a bag to carry the birds and animals she shot. And she always took her dog, a trusted water spaniel that helped Martha retrieve her specimens.

Some people were shocked that Martha could kill birds and animals. "You fearful woman!" a friend once said to her. "How can you have the heart to take so many lives?"

"I suppose you think me very cruel," Martha replied, "but I doubt if I am so much as you! There isn't a day you don't tacitly consent to have some creature killed that you may eat it. I never take life for such carnivorous purposes! All must die some time; I only shorten the period of consciousness that I may give their forms a perpetual memory; and, I leave it to you, which is the more cruel? To kill to eat, or kill ot *immortalize?*"

Between 1868 and 1870, Martha made a number of trips into the mountains. James usually went with her on these camping trips. Sometimes Mary and Mabel went, too. One trip took them to the Black Hills in the Dakota Territory.

In the Black Hills, Martha saw a large herd of antelope feeding beside a lake. She knew that antelope were fast animals and very skittish. To get close to the antelope, Martha tied a piece of red cloth to the end of her **ramrod** and began to crawl toward the herd. The trick worked. The animals were so distracted by the red cloth that they didn't notice Martha. She was able to get close enough to shoot one for her collection.

As Martha skinned the antelope, she measured its height and length. She measured its neck and shoulders as well. With large animals like antelope, Martha took between fifteen and twenty measurements. She also cleaned the bones she needed. It was difficult and dirty work, but Martha always wanted to do everything herself.

It allowed her to study the animal's body and see how all the muscles fit together.

Through trial and error, Martha learned how to prepare large specimens for display. After skinning and measuring the animal, Martha built a model in the shape of its body. At first, she used plaster or clay to build these models. Later, she hired a blacksmith to build an iron frame. She then covered the frame with wool and cotton to make the model soft. After that, she attached the animal's skull and leg bones. Finally, she draped the skin over the model, pulled it tight, and sewed it all in place.

Martha had discovered a way to make her large animals look just as beautiful and realistic as her birds. She didn't know it at the time, but she was one of the first taxidermists to use such a technique. Eventually, all taxidermists would use this technique to prepare large animals.

Martha was earning a reputation as a fine taxidermist. Her specimens were beautiful and lifelike, and she presented them in realistic poses that told a story. People brought their animals to her and paid Martha to prepare them. Taxidermy was no longer a hobby for Martha. Now it was a full-time profession.

When she again exhibited her collection at the Colorado Agricultural Society Fair in 1869, she had more than six hundred specimens—wolves, foxes, mountain lions, wild cats, antelope, deer, weasels, squirrels, badgers, eagles, and hawks of all kinds. Martha had come close to

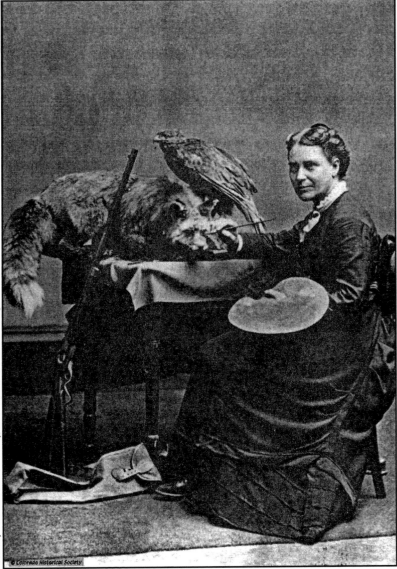

By 1870 Martha's talent was well known. She was now a professional taxidermist with more than 600 specimens in her collection.

her goal of collecting all the native animals and birds of Colorado.

Once again, Martha won a prize for her exhibit at the fair. Mary wrote that Martha's collection "attracted the attention of the leading men in the Territory." They promised Martha that if she showed her collection at the Territorial Fair in Denver, they would pay for her to attend a fair in St. Louis, Missouri. Martha agreed.

In the summer of 1870, Martha traveled to St. Louis with her collection. The fair was held at the famous Shaw's Garden. The fair in St. Louis was much bigger than the one in Denver, with more exhibits and spectators. Martha was thrilled to have so many people see her work. Once again, her exhibit attracted a lot of attention.

While she was in St. Louis, a man from Shaw's Garden offered to buy her entire collection for six hundred dollars. It was a difficult decision for Martha. She had become quite attached to her collection. Not only was she proud of her work, but it represented her contribution to natural history. Still, Martha knew she could always collect more specimens. She accepted the man's offer and sold her collection which went on display at Shaw's Garden museum.

With the money from the sale of her collection, the Maxwells bought land at the mouth of Boulder Canyon. James moved a house there that had been next to his lumbermill. "The situation was an admirable one for a naturalist," Mary said, "as it was visited by animals from both the mountain ranges and the plains." Next to the house, James built a large workshop for Martha She immediately set out to rebuild her collection.

As often as she could, Martha journeyed to the mountains in search of animals and birds. For the species that were hard to find, Martha sometimes had to travel a long way and camp overnight with only her dog for a

*From her home in Boulder Canyon, Martha could hunt both prairie and mountain animals. The Maxwells moved to this house in Boulder in 1871.*

*Martha designed and made her own hunting outfit. The outfit included a jacket, overskirt, and trousers.*

companion. When she went in search of large animals—such as deer and bear—she took a wagon and a team of horses. Sometimes James went with her, especially when Martha needed help loading large animals onto the wagon. She often brought a wire cage so she could trap smaller animals and bring them home alive.

Martha knew how important it was to wear comfortable clothes in the mountains, so she designed her own hunting outfit. She started with a pair of bloomer-like trousers and a medium-length overskirt. Then she made a jacket to keep her warm. She sewed the entire outfit from the same brown-and-checked material. For shoes, she wore hobnailed boots that laced up to her knees. She also wore a wide-brimmed hat to protect her from the sun.

Martha had first seen bloomers when she was a student at Lawrence. She noticed right away how practical they were compared to the corsets, bodices, and long skirts that most women wore. Bloomers also came to symbolize freedom for women, and she liked that.

When Martha was at home, she spent long hours in the workshop preparing her specimens. Her workshop was filled with all the materials she used in her taxidermy: wire, cotton, hay, plaster, iron, and wood. She kept her paints and brushes in one corner of the room. For her habitat displays, she collected mosses, grasses, tree branches, bird nests, and freshwater shells. She stored her guns and ammunition in the shed, too. And, of course, there were the specimens: insects, reptiles, birds, fossils, bones, skins, and the heads and antlers of antelope, mountain sheep, deer, and elk. Mary called the workshop Martha's birdhouse. James called it her den.

Martha liked to keep live animals around so she could study their habits and movements. Some of the animals were caged, while others roamed free. Many learned to respond to her voice. Even the rattlesnakes raised their heads when Martha spoke to them. Martha kept an antelope that liked to walk inside the house and eat the plants. She kept a porcupine named Yocko who stood on its hind legs to beg for food. Martha had to be careful not to get stuck by Yocko's quills when petting him.

A goshawk once flew into the barn and attacked one of the Maxwell's roosters. Martha was able to capture the large bird. She had never trapped a hawk before, so this was her chance to study one up close. She wrapped a rope around its legs and tied it to a large antler in her workshop.

Two days later, Martha checked on the hawk. When she opened the door, there were feathers and stuffing all over the floor. Her bird specimens were in shambles. The goshawk had gotten free and attacked all the stuffed birds in the shed.

Martha managed to rebuild her entire collection of birds and animals. She was most proud of her large animals: deer, elk, antelope, black bear, buffalo, and a grizzly that stood over six feet tall.

*Martha prepared and mounted hundreds, if not thousands, of birds and animals. These shelves hold a few of the bird specimens displayed in her Rocky Mountain Museum in Boulder.*

In October 1871, Martha showed her rebuilt collection at the Boulder County Agricultural Society Fair. Her displays presented the animals and birds in their natural habitats. Martha's exhibit was recognized at the fair as the "Best Collection of Stuffed Birds, Reptiles, and Animals."

# 7 The Rocky Mountain Museum

Martha's collection grew so large that she ran out of room to store it all. Her stuffed birds and animals were in every room of the house. The workshop was full, too. Meanwhile, James's business was not doing well, and the Maxwells needed money. Mabel would soon be starting college. Martha wanted her daughter to attend college, and this would require extra income.

Martha had an idea. She would open a museum. She could store all her specimens in a museum, plus she could charge admission and make money. A museum would also allow people to see Colorado's birds and animals up close. Children could learn from the museum exhibits and perhaps become more interested in natural history.

Martha began planning right away. She collected species that she didn't already have. She looked for other things that she could put in the museum, such as petrified wood, shells, Indian artifacts, and samples of minerals and ores. She hired a geologist to help her collect special rocks from all over Colorado.

Martha's interest in nature went beyond the Colorado Territory. She figured people would like to see things from other places, too. In the summer of 1873, she took a trip to California. She visited San Francisco and hiked among the great sequoia trees. In a letter home, Martha described the sequoia forest. "It is to me the most enchanting place I ever visited, and no language can describe the *magnificence* of that *solitude*."

Martha spent six months in California, traveling and collecting things for her museum—Japanese tea sets, rare coins, even a shark's jaw. She was all set to leave when she saw an ancient suit of armor for sale. Martha wanted the armor for her museum, so she traded her train ticket for a cheaper fare in a boxcar. It was an uncomfortable ride back to Colorado, but she had what she wanted.

Martha hoped to open her museum in Denver. She thought she could earn more money there since more people lived in Denver than Boulder. But rent was too high in Denver, and she couldn't find a room she liked. So, she rented the second floor of the Dabney-Macky building in downtown Boulder. She and James hauled the specimens from their house and opened the museum in June 1874.

A Boulder newspaper reported the grand opening. "The event of the week was the opening of the Rocky Mountain Museum—an event celebrated with flags and music, as befitted an occasion so significant of benefit to this country. The Boulder Brass band and the string band were out. The exhibition itself created quite a sensation; the collection and curiosities and specimens being unexpectedly full and fine."

Martha charged twenty-five cents for admission and greeted everyone at the door. News quickly spread about the interesting exhibit in Boulder. Helen Hunt Jackson, the well-known writer, visited the museum and wrote an article about it for a New York newspaper. "You whosoever visits Boulder and goes away without seeing this museum," she wrote, "loses one of the most interesting and characteristic things in Colorado."

The museum had three rooms. In the front room, Martha made a study area with a table where people could read about natural history. She placed a deer beside the table, "in as easy and natural a position as if he had just walked in," Mrs. Jackson wrote.

Mrs. Jackson described the next room. "The first thing upon which my eyes fell was a black-and-tan terrier, lying on a mat. Not until after a second or two did the strange stillness of the creature suggest to me that it was not alive. Even after I had stood close by its side I could hardly believe it."

The dog's name was Pills. Pills's owner had paid Martha to stuff his pet, but he never returned to pick it up. Martha found a place for the little dog in her museum.

Martha also placed a buffalo in this room. Mrs. Jackson wrote: "In the opposite corner was a huge bison, head down, forefeet planted wide apart and at a slant, eyes viciously glaring at the door—as distinct a charge as ever bison made. Next to him, on a high perch, was a huge eagle, flying with outstretched wings, carrying in his claws the limp body of a lamb."

Above the eagle and lamb, there were stuffed owls on a shelf. Martha also kept two live owls in a cage. "Mrs. Maxwell opened the cage and let them out," Mrs. Jackson wrote. "One of them flew instantly up to its companions on the shelf, perched itself solemnly in the row, and sat there motionless, except for now and then lolling its head to right or left."

Cabinets in the room held some of the curiosities Martha had collected—a reindeer hide from Alaska, war clubs from New Zealand, a silk shoe from China, Japanese vases, kimonos, and swords. In other cabinets were Indian leggings, bows, arrows, and ancient bones and skulls.

The highlight of the museum was the "Bird and Beast" room. With James's help, Martha had built a wooden platform in a corner. She piled rocks and dirt on the platform and planted small trees until the display looked like a mountain with a cave. She placed animal and bird

*Martha wanted people to see her specimens in their natural settings.*
*She and James built a mountain and placed the animals in lifelike poses on it.*
*The mountain display was recreated at the Philadelphia Centennial Exhibition.*

specimens on the mountain according to where they lived in the wild. On the lower part of the mountain, she placed jackrabbits, antelope, owls, rattlesnakes, and prairie dogs. She placed larger animals higher on the mountain.

People came from all over to see Martha's museum, including many famous people. Ferdinand V. Hayden, the noted geologist and **surveyor**, toured the museum and said that Martha's collection "excelled every other in the West." Julia Ward Howe, famous for writing "The Battle Hymn of the Republic," wrote an article about Martha for the *Woman's Journal*.

It was an exciting time for Martha. Her museum had become a success, and she had met famous people. While the museum attracted many visitors, Martha and James knew they could make more money if they moved the museum to Denver. When a man named John H. Pickel offered to pay the rent on a building in Denver, they moved the collection to Lawrence Street.

Martha set up the exhibit in Denver the same way she had in Boulder, only this time she built the mountain twice as high. The cave was bigger—big enough for her to walk through. Martha and James spent most of their time in the museum, even sleeping in the cave at night.

Meanwhile, the nation was getting ready to celebrate its one hundredth birthday. A large exposition was planned in Philadelphia as part of the centennial celebration. Each state and territory would have an exhibit on display. Martha was asked to display her collection of Colorado animals and birds there.

The exhibition was scheduled to open in May. She and James had just moved the museum to Denver. Now they would have to pack and ship everything again. But she could not pass up this opportunity to represent Colorado at the nation's Centennial Exposition. James helped her pack the specimens, and soon Martha was on her way to Philadelphia.

# 8 The Centennial Exposition

When Martha arrived in Philadelphia, everyone was preparing for the big celebration. The city had built an enormous fairground at Fairmount Park, where each state had its own pavilion. The Kansas-Colorado pavilion was one of the biggest state buildings at the exposition.

Martha quickly went to work constructing the mountain and cave for her exhibit. High on the mountain, she put a pipe to provide water for a stream. The stream ran down the mountain and collected in a pool that looked like a lake. She planted tufts of grass and small pine trees around the lake. Then she placed bears, mountain sheep, and cougars on the mountain. She was careful to position the specimens according to where the animals lived in nature. Martha also built a plains habitat to display bison, elk, and antelope. She put live fish in the pool, and turtles, beavers, and muskrats along its edges. As she had in Colorado, Martha included live prairie dogs and rattlesnakes in the exhibit.

While she worked, many people stopped to ask her questions.

"Madam! Could you tell me what is the design of this work?"

"Mrs. will you tell me the name of the animal you have your hands on, and what are you making here?"

"If you please, miss, are these all Kansas critters?"

It took two weeks for Martha to finish building her exhibit. All that was left to do was to give the exhibit a name. Martha wanted people to know that a woman had made all this. She wrote "Woman's Work" on a small sign and placed it in front of her display.

The Centennial Exposition opened on May 10, 1876. President Ulysses S. Grant opened the exposition along with Emperor Dom Pedro of Brazil. Thousands of people came to the fairgrounds that day to see the many marvels on display. Martha's exhibit attracted a lot of attention. She had over a hundred animals and nearly four hundred birds on display.

It was difficult for many visitors to tell the live animals from the stuffed ones. When the emperor visited Martha's exhibit, he whistled at Pills to get the dog's attention. Another man prodded a turtle with his cane. Everyone laughed when the man realized the turtle was not alive.

THE CENTENNIAL.—KANSAS AND COLORADO B

*This drawing of the interior of the Kansas-Colorado Building of the Philadelphia Centennial Exhibition was published June 17, 1876, in Harper's Weekly.*

IT.—From a Sketch by C. E. H. Bonwill.—[See Page 490.]

*Martha had more than 100 animals and nearly 400 birds on display. In front of her exhibit, she placed as sign that read, "Woman's Work."*

One person asked if the dirt on the mountain was real Rocky Mountain soil. Another asked if the Rocky Mountains were much higher than the mountain Martha had built for the exhibit. One woman held a pail under the stream that ran down the mountain. "Try the Colorado water," she told her friends.

As much as everyone enjoyed the lifelike specimens, they were also interested in Martha. Once people learned that she had hunted most of the animals herself, they tried to imagine her with a shotgun in the wilds of Colorado. People wanted to know, "Is she married?" "Did she kill all those animals?" "How did she stuff 'em?" "Does she live in that cave?" "Is she an Indian?"

Mary visited Martha at the exposition and tried to answer some of their questions. She later wrote, "There was never an hour, through all the summer, when there were not numbers of interesting and appreciative people eager to know all about her and her adventures."

Word spread about Martha and her exhibit of birds and animals. Newspaper reporters from all over the country interviewed her. One Philadelphia reporter wrote, "If there is any one person who at such a place as an international exhibition can be regarded as the observed of all observers, it is Mrs. Maxwell." Everyone wanted to know about the "Colorado Huntress." And everyone wanted to take a photograph of Martha dressed in her hunting costume and holding her rifle.

Martha made quite a splash at the exposition. The Kansas and Colorado commissioners presented her with a new Evans magazine rifle. She thanked them and said, "The use of this rare gift shall be directed by a love of science, and in the pursuit of objects for the study of natural history it shall be my trusted companion and assistant." Later that summer, the Centennial Committee honored Martha with a special medal.

As a result of her new fame, Martha was invited to the Philadelphia Academy of Science and Natural History, where she met many scientists. She became friends with Elliot Coues, one of the nation's most important **ornithologists**. Dr. Coues said that Martha's specimens were "mounted in a manner far superior to ordinary museum work."

Martha was thrilled by all the attention, but she knew she needed to make as much money as she could at the exposition. By September, she had saved enough money to support Mabel at college for two years. Mabel had enrolled at Oberlin College in 1874, but she was not happy there and wanted to attend the University of Michigan. While Martha was disappointed that her daughter wanted to leave Oberlin, she was happy that Mabel was at least continuing her college education.

When the exhibition closed in November, Martha decided to move to Washington, D.C., where she could show her collection. James wanted her to return to

Colorado, but Martha felt it was best for her career to stay in the East. "I feel that my life is but just commenced!" she wrote to Mary, "and I want to use it to the best advantage in all ways."

# 9 On the Plains, and Among the Peaks

Mrs. Maxwell's Colorado Centennial Exhibit opened in Washington on December 21, 1876. The *Washington Gazette* ran an article that read, "No one should fail to see this work of ingenious skill and untiring labor."

In spite of the praise, the exhibit did not draw the crowds Martha had hoped it would. To make matters worse, Martha had not been paid her travel expenses to Philadelphia by the Colorado commissioners, as they had promised. To add to her worries, James was unhappy that Martha was in Washington. He wrote and urged her to sell the collection and return to Colorado where she could lobby the state legislature to get the money she was owed. She could then use the money to build a collection for the new university in Boulder.

Again, Martha decided to stay in the East. The exposition had given her the hope that she might succeed financially in her career as a naturalist.

Martha's sister Mary was now married and living in Boston. Ever since she was a little girl in Wisconsin, Mary wanted to be a writer. The two sisters came up with a plan. Together they would write a book about Martha's Life and work. If they could publish the book, it would be good for both of their careers. Martha liked the idea. While Mary wrote a sketch of Martha's life, Martha arranged to have catalogs written for her animals and birds.

Since she first began in taxidermy, Martha had exchanged letters with two scientists at the Smithsonian Institution, Spencer Baird and Robert Ridgway. In Washington, Martha visited Mr. Ridgway and told him about her plans for a book. She asked him to write a catalog for her bird collection. Ridgway agreed. In return, he asked to see Martha's field notes on a group of birds he was studying called the rosy finches. Martha was happy to share her notes with a friend. At the same time, Dr. Coues agreed to write a catalog for Martha's animal collection.

Martha decided to close the exhibit in Washington and return to Philadelphia, where she could display her collection at the "Permanent Exhibition" in the Centennial's Main Building. Once again, Martha's exhibit received good reviews in the newspapers. When the exhibition closed for the season in 1877, Martha needed somewhere to spend the winter. She did not want to return to Colorado. She wrote to Mabel saying she had received "several *unpleasant* letters" from James. "I'm tired of such letters," Martha told her daughter.

In 1878, Martha moved to Boston to be near Mary. There she took classes in biology, chemistry, and mineralogy at the Woman's Laboratory of the Massachusetts Institute of Technology. At age forty-six, Martha still loved to learn. "I am enjoying my studies here very much indeed," she wrote to Josiah. She told him that there were "many wonderful discoveries to be made in science especially in its connection with the R[ocky] M[ountains]."

Martha was able to visit Mary and work on the book. She also arranged for Mabel to attend Wellesley—a new women's college in Boston. Martha visited the New England Woman's Club, one of the most important women's organizations in the nation. Julia Ward Howe was a member. She had written a magazine article about Martha years before. The club invited Martha to speak. Martha considered it a great honor to speak before such a distinguished audience.

Meanwhile, James was becoming more frustrated with Martha. He wrote to her that it was not proper for a "wife and mother to settle herself in a distant city or country among utter strangers away from her husband and home."

Martha felt she had to make a choice between her marriage and her career. She decided to stay in the East to pursue her love of science.

In the summer of 1878, Martha moved back to Philadelphia to reopen her exhibit. There she received a letter from an old Colorado friend, Nathan Meeker, one of the centennial commissioners. Meeker was an Indian agent at the White River Agency in northwestern Colorado. He invited Martha to work at the agency as a teacher. She declined, and it was lucky that she did. The following year, Meeker and other workers at the agency were massacred by a group of Ute Indians.

From Philadelphia that summer, Martha wrote letters to the University of Colorado, asking them to buy her collection of Colorado animals and birds. It was one of Martha's dreams to build a complete collection of bird and animal species native to Colorado. If the university bought her collection, she would have the money and time to finish the project. The university decided not to accept her offer.

Martha and Mary continued to work on the book. Martha told her sister everything she could remember about her life, and Mary wrote it all down in longhand— over four hundred pages of stories, facts, and memories. They called the book *On the Plains, and Among the Peaks; or; How Mrs. Maxwell Made Her Natural History Collection.* The book was published in 1879. At the end of the book,

Mary wrote, "If this story of her adventures shall stimulate any one to a deeper love of her favorite study, whatever her future may be, she will deem her past a success."

*On the Plains* included the catalogs written by Ridgway and Dr. Coues. Dr. Coues told a story about the rare black-footed ferret. James Audubon, the famous American naturalist, first reported seeing this animal in 1851. Because no other scientist had seen it, many people wondered if the animal really existed. After Martha sent three specimens of the ferret to the Smithsonian, scientists finally accepted that the black-footed ferret was real.

In his catalog of Martha's birds, Ridgway praised Martha for her skills as a taxidermist and naturalist. He had a story to tell about Martha, too. When she was in Colorado, she sent him a specimen of a gray owl that she had hunted. Martha could not identify the owl and asked him for help. Ridgway wrote back that no one had ever seen this owl before. Martha had discovered a new **subspecies** of screech owl!

Ridgway named the bird *Scop asio maxwellia,* in Martha's honor. In Latin, this means "Mrs. Maxwell's owl." Martha became the first American woman to discover a bird that was later named after her. Ridgway wrote that the owl was named for her "not only as a compliment to an accomplished and amiable lady, but also as a deserved tribute to her high attainments in the study of natural history."

*On the Plains* earned good reviews. Many professional scientists praised Martha's accomplishments. Spencer Baird said that Martha deserved "the highest credit for what she has done in the way of bringing together a complete representation of mammals and birds of Colorado." Joel Allen, one of America's leading ornithologists, said that Martha provided new scientific knowledge on the habits and distribution of birds. Allen described her centennial exhibit as a "startling revelation of what a woman can do in one of the most difficult fields of art."

Martha stayed in the East, determined to pursue her career as a naturalist. Unfortunately, her money problems continued. In spite of her hard work, she could never seem to make enough money to settle down. For three years, she had moved from city to city. "I'm as lonesome as a stray dog," she wrote to Mary.

In 1879, Martha came up with another idea to make money. She leased a plot of land on Rockaway Beach—a popular seaside resort on Long Island, New York. She built a museum on the plot where she planned to show her exhibit and sell refreshments the next summer. In the meantime, she lived in an apartment in what her sister Mary called a "very poor dirty part of Brooklyn."

In the spring of 1880, Mabel came from Colorado, where she had a teaching job, to help with the new business. She and Martha worked through the summer in Rockaway. While the museum didn't make as much money as she wanted, Martha was determined to try again the next summer.

Martha always hoped that her daughter would follow in her footsteps and become a naturalist, but now she doubted that Mabel would ever be serious about a career. In a letter to Mary, Martha said she was worried about Mabel. "Poor dear victim of vanity and slave to fashion…. Poor child poor Child! I see nothing but unhappiness for her in future—the love of dress has ruined her."

It seemed all Mabel wanted to do was get married and be a homemaker. Her mother had a different view of marriage. For Martha, marriage had meant a lot of hard work that took her away from her interests in taxidermy and the natural world.

"Mother did not understand," Mabel later wrote. "What did I want? A home, I told her. All my life I longed for a home and I had never had one. The feminist in mother protested fiercely. What about a career? Making a home, I retorted seemed to me the finest and most useful career a woman could have."

When Mabel became engaged to Dr. Charles Brace of Boulder, Martha wrote to her sister, "My ambition for her has been crushed."

Martha spent the winter alone in Brooklyn. Her health was failing; she had little energy and often fainted. In April 1881, she received the sad news that Josiah had died. Not long afterward Mabel came to New York to be with her sick mother. Mabel sent for a doctor, who told Martha that she was dying of cancer. Mabel and Martha put their differences aside. "Mother was so pitifully glad to see me that it almost broke my heart," Mabel wrote.

On May 31, 1881, Martha died in Mabel's arms. She was forty-nine years old.

# Martha's Legacy

Martha Maxwell lived a remarkable life. She grew up on the frontier in Pennsylvania and Wisconsin. She traveled west on the Oregon Trail and worked in the Colorado mining camps. Later, she became a famous taxidermist and naturalist. She was the first woman field naturalist to collect and prepare her own animal and bird specimens.

Martha influenced the way natural history museums displayed birds and animals. People liked Martha's birds and animals because they were beautiful and realistic. They also liked the way she displayed them in their natural habitats. Martha was one of the first taxidermists to do this.

Through her museums in Boulder and Denver, Martha became well known as an expert on Colorado animals and Philadelphia made her famous across the country. Many newspaper and magazine articles were written about her.

Martha's life was not the easy life of a successful celebrity. Earning enough money from taxidermy was always a challenge. She was not happy in her marriage, and her relationship with her daughter was often troubled. James and Mabel wanted Martha to be a homemaker. Martha struggled to meet the needs of her family and do what made her happy at the same time. She was a gifted taxidermist who took her art seriously. The woman Helen Hunt Jackson described as a "wee, modest, tenderhearted woman as shy as one of her weasels" achieved much success in her remarkable life and became a role model for women who wished to follow their dreams.

# Timeline

1831 – Martha Ann Dartt is born in Dartt's Settlement, Pennsylvania.

1845 – Martha's family moves to Wisconsin, where they later settle in Baraboo.

1851 – Martha enrolls at Oberlin College and attends classes for one year.

1854 – Martha marries James Maxwell in Appleton, Wisconsin.

1857 – Mabel Maxwell is born to Martha and James.

1860 – Martha and James travel the Oregon Trail on their wat to the goldfields of Colorado.

1862 – Martha returns to Baraboo where she begins to learn taxidermy.

1867 – Martha moves to Vineland, New Jersey.

1868 – Martha rejoins James in Boulder, Colorado. She shows her display of birds at the Colorado Agricultural Society exhibition in Denver.

1870 – Martha exhibits her collection at the Shaw's Garden in St. Louis.

1874 – Martha's Rocky Mountain Museum opens in Boulder.

1876 – Martha opens her exhibit at the Centennial Exhibition in Philadelphia.

1877 – The Smithsonian Institution publishes a catalog of birds that includes a Rocky Mountain screech owl discovered by Martha.

1879 – *On the Plains* is published. Written by her sister Mary, the book tells the story of Martha's life.

1880 – Martha opens a museum at a seaside resort in Rockaway Beach, New York.

1881 – Martha dies in Brooklyn, New York.

# Glossary

**activism** – the practice of being involved in social or political causes

**anatomy** – the structure of a plant or animal's body

**boardinghouse** – a house at which meals and lodging may be obtained for payment

**chaperone** – to accompany young people in public to ensure proper behavior

**Civil War** – the war between the northern and southern states of the United States fought in the years 1861 to 1865

**Conestoga wagon** – a broad-wheeled covered wagon used during early westward expansion, usually drawn by six horses

**depression** – a time of economic hardship when business and employment are at low levels

**Dutch oven** – a metal utensil used for baking over a fire, fitted with shelves

**habitat** – the place where a plant or animal **species** naturally lives and grows

**melodeon** – a keyboard musical instrument

**missionary** – a person sent into a newly settled or foreign region to carry on religions work

**natural history** – the study of nature—plants, animals, and minerals—especially from an amateur or popular point of view

**ornithology** – the study of birds

**ramrod** – a cleaning rod for the barrel of a rifle; also, a rod used in ramming home the charge of a muzzle-loading firearm

**reform** – the improvement of what is wrong or corrupt through a new course of action or behavior

**sanitarium** – a hospital for the treatment of diseases or mental sickness through rest, exercise, diet, and therapy

**scarlet fever** – a contagious disease that causes a fever and a red rash

**scavenger** – an animal or bird that feeds on dead or decaying matter

**sod house** – a house with walls built of sod or turf cut from the earth and laid in horizontal layers

**species** – a group of plants or animals with common characteristics that is capable of producing offspring

**squatter's claim**– a legal claim to a piece of land earned through continuous occupation

**stake a claim** – a mining practice whereby a miner claims a right to occupy and mine a tract of land according to conditions prescribed by law

**subspecies** – a subdivision of a species usually associated with a specific area or habitat

**surveyor** – one who measures an area of land for size, shape, or the position of boundaries

**taxidermy** – the art of stuffing and mounting the skins of animals and birds

**trousseau** – accumulation of clothes, accessories, and household good usually acquired in preparation for marriage

# For Further Study

**VISIT** The Colorado Historical Society, 1300 Broadway, Denver, Colorado.

**VISIT** The Carnegie Branch Library for Local History, 1125 Pine Street, Boulder, Colorado.

**VISIT** The Boulder Museum of History, 1206 Euclid Avenue, Boulder, Colorado.

**READ** Benson, Maxine. *Martha Maxwell, Rocky Mountain Naturalist.* Lincoln: University of Nebraska Press, 1986.

**READ** Thompson, Mary Dartt. *On the Plains, and Among the Peaks; or; How Mrs. Maxwell Made Her Natural History Collection.* Philadelphia: Claxton, Remsen and Haffelfinger, 1879 [1878].

# Bibliography

Benson, Maxine. "Colorado Celebrates the Centennial, 1876." *Colorado Magazine.* 53/2 Spring 1976, 129-152.

Benson, Maxine. *Martha Maxwell, Rocky Mountain Naturalist.* Lincoln: University of Nebraska Press, 1986.

Brace, Mabel Maxwell. *Thanks to Abigail: A Family Chronicle.* n.p. privately published, 1948.

Ellis, Carrie Scott. "A Stuffy Subject." *The 1960 Brand Book, Being Volume Sixteen of the Denver Posse of the Westerners.* Ed. Guy M. Herstrom, 287-310.

Felger, A. H. "Bibliography of Mrs. M.A. Maxwell, Pioneer Naturalist of Colorado."Unpublished manuscript.

Howe, Julia Ward. *Woman's Journal.* February 27, 1875, 65.

Jackson, Helen Hunt. "Bits of Travel at Home: Mrs. Maxwell's Museum." *Bounder* County *News*, October 15, 1875. Also *New York Independent*, September 23, 1875.

Martha Maxwell Collection. Colorado Historical Society, Denver.

Melrose, Frances. "Rockies 'Huntress' Was Early Feminist." *Rocky Mountain News*, July 2, 1989.

Stryker, George W. "Martha Maxwell Developed in Boulder Natural Habitats for Displays Later Adopted By National History Museums." *Boulder Daily Camera*, July 3, 1954.

Thompson, Mary Dartt. *On the Plains, and Among the Peaks; or, How Mrs. Maxwell Made Her Natural History Collection*. Philadelphia: Claxton, Remsen and Haffelfinger, 1876 [1878].

# Index

# Acknowledgments

This book was made possible in part by funds provided by the University of North Carolina at Charlotte. I would especially like to thank Mark I. West for starting me on this project. This book could not have been written without the valuable assistance from librarians at the Colorado Historical Society, the Carnegie Branch Library for Local History in Boulder, and the University of Colorado Library Archives.

Two people helped me prepare the final manuscript—Susan Booker and Kathleen Phillips. My appreciation goes to both of them.

I would also like to thank my nieces and nephews who assistd in the editing process: Barbara Burke, Emily Burke, Douglas Burke, Jack McVey, and Jim McVey. Finally, I would like to acknowledge my son, Kyle, the joy of my life.

# About the Author

James McVey was born in Ohio and grew up in northern Michigan. He earned a master's degree in environmental science and worked briefly as a wildlife biologist in the Adirondack Mountains. He earned a doctorate in English at the University of Colorado, where he teaches creative writing and Americn literature. His short stories and outdoor essays have appeared in literary journals around the country. His first book, *The Wild Upriver and Other Stories,* was published in 2005 by Arbutus Press.